What's a man's ide
housework?

Lifting his legs so yc

What do you have to do to keep a man interested?

Wear perfume that smells like beer.

~

What's the difference between a man and E.T.?

E.T. phoned home.

~

Why is it good that there are female astronauts?

When the crew gets lost in space, at least the women will ask for directions.

~

What does a man consider a 7 course meal?

A hot dog and a 6 pack.

. . . Look inside for even more jokes about men

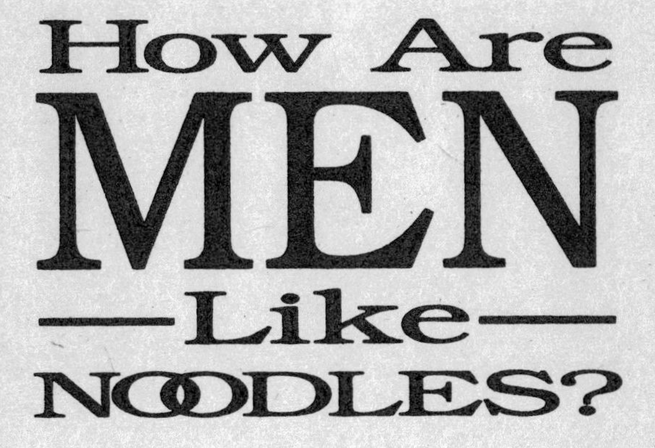

The
Ultimate Jokebook
About Men

CINDY GARNER

Newport House, Inc.

More Humor Books from Newport House

Everything Men Know about Women

Sex after 60

77 Uses for an Ex

MEN! The Cartoon Book

Newport House, Inc.
107 R.R. 620 S., Suite 7-A
Austin, TX 78734

How Are Men Like Noodles? / Cindy Garner
First Newport House edition, 1991.

Designed and typeset by Michele Lanci-Altomare

Manufactured in the United States of America

ISBN 0-939515-14-8

Thanks to these writers and friends for their contributions:

J.W. Moore, Kathy Borne, Angela Ross, Linda Perret, Beverly Hershfield, Edie Schiffendecker, Pam L., Marian Moskowitz, Carolyn Kellams, Erick, Leanna Wolfe, R. Dickert, Margie Kelly, Jean Moore, J. Kriwiel, Jenefer Denberg, Annetta Darrough, P. Miller, D.J. Boone, B. Pugh, N. Wolkoff, Theresa Frohman, E. O'Brien, Sue Sebesta, T. Padovano, M. Milliken, Donna Kress, J. McBride, Debra Mancuso, and Doris Lee McCoy.

To my mother, who is a joy
and inspiration

And to Sandy, who has always
believed in me

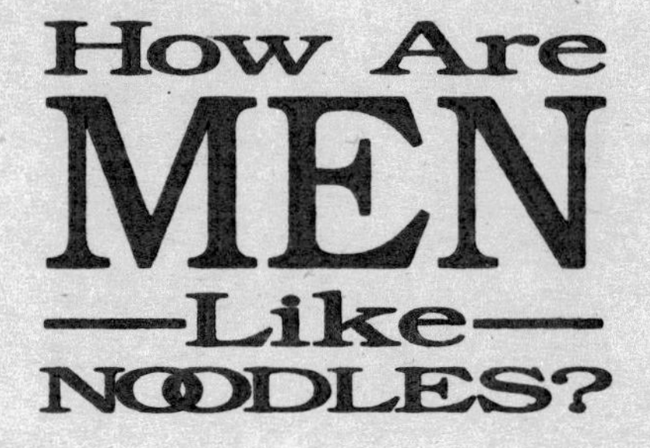
How Are
MEN
Like
NOODLES?

CONTENTS

ROMANCE

~

What's a man's definition of a romantic evening?

Sex.

~

What is the only time a man thinks about a candlelight dinner?

When the power goes off.

~

Why do men like frozen dinners?

They like being able to both eat and make love in under 3 minutes.

~

My husband has always taken the time to make love to me in a very romantic atmosphere. In fact, all our kids were conceived during Miller Lite commercials.

~

Why would we women be better off if men treated us like cars?

At least then we'd get a little attention every 6 months or 50,000 miles, whichever came first.

~

What's a man's idea of a romantic gift that is also practical?

A toaster that glows in the dark.

~

A woman is getting a sentimental feeling while watching a beautiful love scene in a movie. Her husband leans over and whispers those three little words that are on his mind: "Pass the popcorn."

~

What do you have to do to keep a man interested?

Wear perfume that smells like beer.

~

When a woman gets married, she expects the three Ss: sensitivity, sincerity, and sharing. What does she get?

The three Bs: burps, body odor, and beer breath.

~

MEN AND WOMEN

~

What's the only exercise most men get at the beach?

Sucking in their stomachs every time they see a bikini.

~

How can a woman find out what life's like without a man around?

Get married.

~

How do men define a 50/50 relationship?

a. We cook/ they eat

b. We iron/ they wrinkle

c. We clean/ they dirty

~

Men will cater to women's needs, so long as what we want is:

a. to have sex

b. to go to a ball game

c. to bring him a beer

~

What do men and women have in common?

They both distrust men.

~

Why is it silly that men accuse women of gossiping?

It's men that give us something to gossip about!

~

Men will do anything for us except:

a. work

b. talk

c. clean up after themselves

~

What's the difference between a pregnant belly and a beer belly?

One gives birth and the other gives burps.

~

How can you tell the difference between men's real gifts and their guilt gifts?

Guilt gifts are nicer.

~

ONE UP ON MEN

~

Diamonds are a girl's best friend. Dogs are man's best friend. Now you know which sex is dumber.

~

Woman conceived Dr. Seuss, Neil Armstrong, and Mother Theresa. What has man contributed to humanity?

He conceived the Edsel, the income tax, and scented kitty litter.

~

Why is it a good thing there are female astronauts?

When the crew gets lost in space, the women will ask for directions.

~

What's the best way to force a man to do sit-ups?

Put the remote control between his toes.

~

A woman's idea of the perfect man is someone who is obedient, well-mannered, and empties the garbage. Now if only you could train a dog to take out the trash...

~

Why do women get depressed more often than men?

They have to put up with men.

~

Man: Since I first laid eyes on you, I've wanted to make love to you in the worst way.

Woman: Well, you succeeded.

~

If they can send one man to the moon, why can't they send them all?

~

An attractive woman in a bikini walked past a husband and wife on the beach. The man noticed his wife was watching him as he stared.

"Just taking a gander," he said.

"Be careful or I'll cook your goose," she replied.

~

They say that men only care about sex. That's not exactly true. They also care a lot about:

a. power and world domination

b. money

c. beer

~

A man leaned toward an attractive woman at a bar and used his best line, "Haven't I seen you somewhere before?" "Yes," she replied in a loud voice, "I'm the receptionist at the V.D. clinic."

~

Why is psychoanalysis a lot quicker for men than women?

When it's time to go back to his childhood, he's already there!

~

What do you instantly know about a well-dressed man?

His wife is good at picking out clothes.

~

Why do men have an inferiority complex?

Because they *are* inferior.

~

WHAT ARE MEN LIKE?

~

How are men like paper cups?

Both are dispensable.

~

How are men like UFO's?

You don't know where they come from, what their mission is, or what time they're going to take off.

~

How is a man like the weather?

Nothing can be done to change either one of them.

~

What's the difference between the average man and E.T.?

E.T. phoned home.

~

How are men like commercials?

You can't believe a word either one says.

~

How are men like blenders?

You know you need one, but you're not quite sure why.

~

How are men like walnuts?

They're hard nuts to crack.

~

How are men like noodles?

a. They're always in hot water.

b. They lack taste.

c. They need dough.

~

How are men like popcorn?

They satisfy you, but only for a little while.

~

How are men and spray paint alike?

One squeeze and they're all over you.

~

How are men like glue?

Once they get stuck on you, you can't shake them off.

~

How is a man and a sports car alike?

Neither one can be depended on and they

both move too fast.

~

What's the difference between a sofa and a man watching Monday Night Football?

The sofa doesn't keep asking for beer.

~

How are boyfriends like cockroaches?

They hang around the kitchen and it's hard to get rid of them.

~

How are men like diplomas?

You spend lots of time getting one, but once you have it you don't know what to do with it.

~

How are men like banana peels?

They're slippery.

~

MEN

~

What popular piece of furniture was named after the typical man?

The La-Z-Boy recliner.

~

Why do many therapists charge men half price?

Because they're so simple to figure out.

~

If men had PMS, what would happen?

a. The federal government would allocate funds to study it.

b. Cramps would become an acceptable reason to apply for permanent disability.

c. There would be a federal holiday every 28 days.

d. All of the above.

~

If women are magnets, what are men?

Scrap metal.

~

If one man can wash one stack of dishes in one hour, how many stacks of dishes can four men wash in four hours?

None. They'll all sit down together and watch football on television.

~

How are men like bras?

They offer light, medium, and complete

support.

~

What is a man's worst nightmare?

a. The Super Bowl is pre-empted by a soap opera

b. His wife has amnesia and forgets how to cook so he has to do it

c. A female boss

d. He has to ask his wife for money.

~

Which of the following is more likely to come when you call?

a. a man

b. a dog

~

A man will never admit he's lost. What will he say?

a. "I'm just taking the scenic route."

b. "They must have changed the streets since I was here last."

~

Why can't we women just let men run the show?

Because they have no script.

~

Wouldn't it be wonderful if there was a potion that could give the average guy the physique of Sylvester Stallone, the brains of Ted Koppel, and the sense of humor of John Goodman? Of course, it could be a little scary. One mix up and you end up with a guy with John Goodman's body, Sylvester Stallone's IQ, and the charm of Ted Koppel.

~

What's the greatest mystery about men?

How they can get older but still manage to remain immature.

~

Single women claim that all the good men are married, while all married women complain about their lousy husbands. This confirms that there is no such thing as a good man.

~

How do you keep a man from wanting sex?

You marry him.

~

How can you tell if a man's playing around?

He sends you a love note that's Xeroxed and begins, "To whom it may concern."

~

What usually happens when a man puts his best foot forward?

It ends up in his mouth.

~

Why are men happy?

Because ignorance is bliss.

~

A man says, “My wife doesn't understand me.” He

a. is on the make.

b. hopes you've never heard that line before.

c. has a wife who understands him only too well.

d. all of the above

~

LOOKS

~

How can you tell if a man has animal magnetism?

He attracts fleas.

~

What happens when a man tries to hide his baldness by combing his hair across his head?

The truth comes shining through.

~

How do most men compare to Tom Cruise?

They have everything he has, except for talent, money, and looks.

~

In our premarital counseling, our therapist talked about how we should keep growing as people. I never dreamed my husband would grow to *250 pounds!*

~

MEN'S DREAMS

~

Women dream of world peace, a safe environment and eliminating hunger. What do men dream of?

Being stuck in an elevator with the Doublemint twins.

~

At the mall, women get excited, thrilled and overjoyed by purchasing the perfect item. Men experience the same thing just by finding a close parking space.

~

If a man were king, he would:

a. make every Sunday Super Bowl Sunday

b. outlaw cleaning

c. require women to work naked

~

DATING

~

How could Will Rogers say, "I never met a man I didn't like"?

He never had to date one.

~

How can you tell if a man you're dating is lazy?

He *throws* his kisses.

~

A single man in his 40's often has a problem finding women at his level of maturity. That's why he dates someone half his age.

~

What do you call a man who expects to have sex on the second date?

Slow.

~

Nowadays, the only place to find the best man is at a wedding.

~

How can you tell it's puppy love?

He slobbers all over you.

~

I never date a guy who has tight jeans. I figure if he can wear tight jeans and still be comfortable, he doesn't have anything in them that would interest me.

~

Why is it good to date men with lots of interests?

They can bore you on dozens of subjects.

~

I'd enjoy my dates a lot better if they *wouldn't* be themselves.

~

Which of these lines will do a better job of frightening men away:

a. "Get away or I'll call a cop."

b. "I love you and want to marry you and have your children."

~

Since I started dating, I have followed one of my mother's quaint old sayings: "Don't pick that up! You don't know where it's been!"

~

I'm going to write a screenplay about the men I've been out with— and call it *Dances with Wolves*.

~

Your date says he's forgotten his wallet and wonders if you could pay for dinner. He is

a. a cheapskate

b. a liar

c. a cheapskate and a liar

d. all of the above

~

BACHELORS

~

Why is going to a singles bar like being a matador?

You have to dodge a lot of bull.

~

What can a woman find at both gyms and singles bars?

Dumbbells.

~

What is the one thing that all men at singles bars have in common?

They're married.

~

What are the only two kinds of men?

Studs and duds.

~

So many bachelors lie about their jobs, drive cars they can't afford, wear toupees and loose shirts that hide their stomachs- and say they want a "real woman"!

~

What's one honest thing most men tell us while courting?

That they aren't good enough for us.

~

We women like to think of ourselves like we're Snow White waiting for the Handsome Prince. But the guys we usually meet are more like Dopey, Grumpy, and Sleepy.

~

If life's a highway, what are most men?

A dead end.

~

Jobs- What single men say (and the truth)

"I work high up in an executive office tower."
(He's a window washer.)

"I work with computers."
(He's a cashier at a self-service gas station.)

"I have the Midas touch."
(He installs mufflers.)

"I'm in television."
(He fixes them.)

"I'm involved in banking."
(He's a guard.)

"I play in the market."
(Safeway)

"My job keeps me running."
(He's a messenger.)

"My business is hot!"
(He hands out towels in a steam room.)

"I'm self-employed."
(He just got fired.)

"I'm a novelist."
(He has 10 unpublished books.)

"I'm consulting."
(He's looking for a job.)

~

Meeting Women- What He Says (and What He Means)

Hello
(Let's have sex)

How are you
(in the sack)

Do you have the time
(to go to bed)

~

Understanding the Personals-
What his Ad says
(and the Truth)

"Looking for a satisfying relationship"
(He wants sex.)

"Wants discreet companionship"
(He wants sex and he's married.)

"Loves opera"
(He wants sex and he's been to the opera once.)

"Responsible male..."
(He wants sex and he's got a job.)

~

COMMITMENT

~

Men most resemble what animal?

Dogs- only they're not as loyal.

~

What do men have difficulty keeping?

a. a job

b. a budget

c. a promise

d. a secret

e. a friendship

f. a marriage

g. all of the above

~

Men would rather pledge allegiance to a flag than to a woman.

~

When there's trouble, can you count on a man?

Yes, you can count on him to be somewhere else.

~

MARRIAGE

~

Marriage for women has its ups and downs. How?

The toilet seat is up and hubby's sex interest is down.

~

What could men do to make their marriages last longer?

Pay less attention to prenuptial agreements and more to postnuptial sex.

~

Why do women cry at weddings?

You'd cry too if you knew the guys they're marrying!

~

Why do men get married?

So they'll have someone to cheat on.

~

Women are marrying men in record numbers. What does this prove?

That women *can* take a joke.

~

How can you tell the married men at a wedding reception?

They're the ones dancing with everyone but their wives.

~

A woman I know is engaged to a real golf nut. They're supposed to get married next

Saturday... but only if it rains.

~

What does marriage teach women?

Patience.

~

My marriage is childless- except for my husband.

~

Why is a driver's license better than a marriage license?

It only lasts 4 years.

~

When a woman gets to the "better or worse" part of the wedding ceremony, she's already experienced the better part.

~

What's a tragedy?

To marry a man for love- and find out he

has no money.

~

Men tell us those three magic words "I love you" while dating. What three magic words replace them after marriage?

"What's for dinner?"

~

Men Before Marriage	**After Marriage**
Gently rubbing me with hot oil	Gently rubbing his car with hot wax
Watching me undress	Watching championship wrestling
Reading poetry	Reading the newspaper
Passionately urging me on	Passionately urging his football team on

~

MARRIED MEN

~

What does a bird's song and a husband have in common?

They're both "cheap."

~

What do you call a husband who is sloppy, spends at least one night a week out with the boys, and never lifts a finger around the house?

About average.

~

When women say that their husband is "well rounded," they're talking about his...

a. education

b. interests

c. belly

~

Even though some husbands work overtime on their jobs, they still enjoy activities in the family room- especially sleeping on the couch.

~

What's the difference between a husband and a gorilla?

The gorilla doesn't leave as much hair in the bath tub.

~

Most husbands don't like to hear their wives struggling with housework- so they turn up the volume on the television.

~

What's the difference between a boyfriend and a husband?

About 30 pounds.

~

Which word does not belong with the others?

a. sensitive

b. affectionate

c. husband

d. polite

~

What do an insensitive husband and an employee at a soda fountain have in common?

They're both jerks.

~

Your husband says he wants to go deer hunting for a week with his friends. He is

a. going to hunt for "dears"

b. going to stay drunk the whole time

c. going to lose all of his money playing poker

d. all of the above

~

Husbands don't like to air dirty linen in public. They'd rather drop it on the floor.

~

How can you tell if a new husband is lazy?

He asks *you* to carry *him* across the threshold!

~

It's difficult after a hard day on the job to come home to a crying demanding little boy, but that's the price a woman pays for having a husband.

~

It's your anniversary. Your husband will

a. forget it.

b. try to convince you that he didn't forget it.

c. show up with flowers and a card the next day.

d. all of the above

~

Matching Questions

___ 1. Sloppy	a. husband
___ 2. Forgets important dates	b. husband
___ 3. Stays out late	c. husband
___ 4. Inconsiderate	d. husband
___ 5. Insensitive	e. husband
___ 6. Stingy	f. husband

~

Fill-in-the-Blanks

The following fill-in-the-blanks will cover most situations in which your husband wants to apologize. First he will say

"Dear, I'm sorry I __________

forgot your birthday."
forgot your anniversary."

acted like an idiot at the party."
got drunk last night."
worked late every night this week."
missed our daughter's recital."
yelled at you."

Then he will ___________

give you candy.
give you flowers.
give you a card.
take you to the movies.
take you to a restaurant.
open a bottle of champagne.

Then he will expect to _________

have sex
have sex
have sex
have sex
have sex
have sex
have sex

~

FAITHFULNESS

~

What does SWM stand for in a personal column advertisement?

Sneaking While Married.

~

What's the difference between a man and an alley cat?

A man is taller.

~

Multiple choice: You meet a charming man at a bar and he asks for your phone number, but claims *he* doesn't have one. He is

a. married

b. married

c. married

d. all of the above

~

A man is caught cheating by his wife and he suggests the fault be shared. What does he mean?

His wife should share the fault with the other woman.

~

Why do men cheat women who trust them?

It's too difficult to cheat women who don't.

~

Married Men/ Single Women- He Says (and the Truth)

I'm divorced.
(I just slipped off my wedding ring.)

My wife doesn't understand me.
(She understands him completely.)

I'll be out of town a few days.
(I'll be in town spending time with my wife and kids.)

I can't leave my wife just now. Be patient.
(Be patient forever.)

~

MY HUSBAND

~

My man has a nautical tattoo on his stomach. It used to be on his chest, but he dropped anchor.

~

Some men have no sense of humor. My man has no sense *and* no humor.

~

He'll go to the gym and bench press 50 pounds 20 times. Then he'll come home and tell me he doesn't have the energy to help me bring in the groceries.

~

My husband is so slow, he has to make instant coffee the night before.

~

My husband is so fat, once he fell asleep on the beach, and three guys tried to roll him back into the ocean!

~

My husband took me to a drive-in, and it was just like it used to be. On the way, he picked up two of his buddies and hid them in the trunk!

~

NO GOOD MEN

~

What does a man notice when he takes a trip to the beach with his girlfriend?

Every other woman there.

~

How do some men avoid making a wrong career move?

They never get a job.

~

The average man:

a. knows every inch of his car, but can't say

the same about his girlfriend.

b. knows the exact date he bought his car, but can't recall his anniversary.

c. can shift gears with a lot more skill in his car than he can in bed.

~

How can you tell when a man is hard to live with?

When even his dog leaves him.

~

What is a "man about town"?

He's here, there, and everywhere- except home.

~

Some men brag, "I've never been fired from a job in my life." This is usually because:

a. he's always quit before they could fire him.

b. he's never *had* a job in his life.

~

What's a man's idea of fairness?

Having his cake and eating yours too.

~

Men will do anything for us except:

a. not fall asleep immediately after sex

b. tell us what's wrong when we ask

c. ask for directions when they're driving

~

Why do many men try to avoid being themselves?

Because they know the truth.

~

How about those girls falling all over Spuds MacKenzie!? I know there's not much out there, but is it really necessary for us women to leave our own *species?!*

~

Many men keep looking and looking for the

right woman. What is really wrong?

They're not the right man!

~

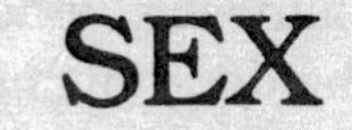

~

How are men like food in a microwave?

30 seconds and they're done.

~

Why don't most women ever tell their husbands when they're enjoying sex?

Because their husbands are never there!

~

What do most men think Mutual Orgasm is?

An insurance company.

~

Most men aren't interested in sex anymore after marriage. In some cases, the situation is so bad that:

a. the husband changes positions more when he's asleep than he does during sex.

b. the husband doesn't go to sleep immediately after sex- he goes to sleep *during* sex

c. If Madonna was married to one of these men, she wouldn't just feel like a virgin, she'd *be* a virgin!

~

What do most women miss most about being single?

Having sex.

~

What's the best way to keep a man happy in bed?

Bring the TV into the bedroom.

~

Men are so indiscriminate about sex. My man filled out an application and under "Sex" he put "Yes".

~

I bought a waterbed, hoping it would improve my husband's sexual performance. It didn't. Now I call it "The Dead Sea."

~

What would we women say if we told the truth in bed?

a. "Was that *it???*"

b. "Getting a little chubby, aren't we?"

c. "*Two minutes!* Boy, that really must have tired you out!"

~

Do most men think women are only good for sex?

No. Most men think they are also good for doing housework.

~

Men like to have the light on during sex. Women prefer the lights off. Some say men are visually-oriented. They like to see what they're getting. Women are visually-oriented too. We know what we're getting, and we'd just as soon not have to see it!

~

What does a man think foreplay is?

a. It's something that you do on the golf course.

b. It's something that occurs 2 minutes before having sex.

~

If men paid as much attention to their women as they do to their cars, Dr. Ruth would be out of business.

~

What should a woman do when her mate refuses a condom because "It cuts down on what I feel"?

Say, "Good, then we'll be even!"

~

Why do a married man and his single male friend envy each other?

Each one thinks the other is having sex more often.

~

The average man wants to:

a. have sex once a day.

b. tell other men that he's having sex once a day.

c. tell other men who are *dumb* enough to believe that he is telling the truth when he says he's having sex once a day.

~

My boyfriend thinks the only safe sex is sitting around talking about it. But, at $2 a minute, it's getting pretty expensive!

~

Singles- Match what a Man Says and Does with What He Wants

1. Says hello	a. sex
2. Asks you out	b. sex
3. Buys you roses	c. sex
4. Buys you dinner	d. sex
5. Takes you to a show	e. sex

~

MEN AND FOOD

~

What does a man consider to be a 7- course meal?

A hot dog and a 6- pack.

~

What do most men consider a gourmet restaurant?

Any place without a drive-up window.

~

The average bachelor *really believes* he is cooking when he:

a. adds milk to a bowl of cereal

b. heats up a slice of pizza in the microwave

c. picks up the phone and orders Chinese food

d. warms up leftovers that his mom put in the refrigerator

~

When dating, the Frenchman in a man compels him to take a woman to expensive restaurants. After marriage, the Scotsman in a man compels him to take his wife to McDonald's.

~

What's a man's favorite meal?

Anything his mother made.

~

Men shouldn't be allowed to cook. Allowing a man in your kitchen is like letting Uncle Buck wallpaper your house.

~

How many men does it take to dirty 10 pots while cooking a meal?

One.

~

MEN AND GOD

~

What did God say after he created man?

I can do better.

~

What one thing did God do right when he created man?

He created woman to explain the difference between his black and navy blue socks.

~

I get the feeling that God not only took

Adam's ribs, but also his brain.

~

My husband's going to have a rude awakening when he gets to Heaven. He'll find out two things: God is a woman... and she nailed all the toilet seats down!

~

Why do so few men end up in heaven?

They never stop to ask for directions.

~

Three men stood before St. Peter.

"I have one question before you go stand in final judgement," St. Peter said. "What do each of you think of women?"

"I was married three times," the first said. "I have no use for them."

"I was married once," the second said, "but all she ever did was nag, nag, nag."

"I can't stand women," the third added. "I remained single my whole life."

"God has about finished with the last group," St. Peter said. "I'll take you in to see *Her* now."

~

MEN AND WORK

~

My man keeps talking about getting our money to work harder. It never occurs to him to get *himself* working harder!

~

What will a man say if you ask him why he failed?

"I give up."

~

What finally gets many men standing on their own two feet?

They miss two car payments and their car gets taken away.

~

My man wasn't affected by the crash of '89. He failed in '88.

~

How do men kid themselves about the future?

They expect to go places, but they won't get out of bed.

~

COMMUNICATING

~

What's the real reason men can't communicate?

It's hard to drink beer and talk at the same time.

~

When do men insist that women are illogical?

When a woman doesn't agree with them.

~

Why don't men show their feelings?

Because they don't *have* feelings.

~

My man talks so much, I have to go to Alanon meetings just to get someone to listen to me.

~

What's the easiest way to get a man to go to sleep?

Say you want to talk to him.

~

Men are so self-centered. At a party I met a guy who talked on and on about himself and then says, "But enough about me, let's talk about you. What do *you* think of *me*?"

~

How do you get a man's attention?

Carry around a TV tuned to sports.

~

At first I thought my guy was the strong, silent type. But lately I've realized- he has nothing to say!

~

He's a great conversationalist, as long as *he's* the subject.

~

His Background- What a Man Says (and the Truth)

"I'm coming off a long relationship."
(My wife is divorcing me.)

"My wife and I are separated."
(She's at home and I'm here.)

"I enjoy reading."
(Playboy and Penthouse)

"I like a woman who is intelligent."
(As long as she acts like I'm smarter.)

"My family is wealthy."
(His 4th cousin has $100 in savings.)

"I've traveled extensively in foreign countries."
(He once got drunk in Tijuana.)

"I'm thinking of relocating."
(He can't find a job locally.)

~

Making Up- He Says
(He Means)

I miss you
(I miss your cleaning up)

I'm sorry
(I'm sorry you caught me)

~

Getting Along- He Says
(He Means)

I'll support you in every way
(except money)

Let's go out wherever you like
(as long as it's cheap)

I'm not ready for a relationship
(with you)

~

MEN'S GENEROSITY

~

How can you tell if a man is cheap?

He turns down the lights... to save money.

~

A woman tells the man in her life she wants to see more of the world. What does he do?

He buys her a globe.

~

After marriage a man would rather pinch a

penny than pinch his wife.

~

When a cheap man gives a woman a gift and tells her it's "worth millions," what has he probably given her?

A lottery ticket.

~

A man doesn't mind sharing his life with a woman- just not his money.

~

When a woman tells her husband she doesn't get out enough in the fresh air, what does he usually do?

He leaves the kitchen door open so that she can feel a breeze while doing the dishes.

~

When a man says he wants to satisfy your every need, he means:

a. as long as it doesn't cost him much money

b. as long as it doesn't take him much time

c. as long as you in return satisfy *his* every need

~

Men are such a bargain. In fact, they're really cheap.

~

My husband's so cheap, he not only reuses tea bags, he saves the string for shoelaces.

~

HANDY-MEN

~

What's a man's idea of helping with the housework?

Lifting his legs so you can vacuum.

~

How many husbands does it take to change a light bulb?

We'll know as soon as one gets off the couch and does it.

~

When it comes to helping around the house,

where do most men stop?

At nothing.

~

How are a husband and a cat similar when it comes to housework?

They're both afraid of the vacuum cleaner.

~

The time a man says, "I do" is generally:

a. the best moment in his life

b. a moment to treasure

c. the last time you'll see him *do* much of anything!

~

Besides "I love you," what three words does a wife want to hear most?

"I'll fix it."

~

I just bought a subliminal tape to play to my husband while he's asleep. It says, "I will help with the housework... I will help with the housework..."

~

What is the only weight lifting most men do in a day?

Lifting themselves out of bed.

~

NEATNESS

~

Where can you find the best selection of men's socks?

On their bedroom floor.

~

How sloppy is the average bachelor's apartment?

a. He thinks he hears a ringing in his ears because it's been months since he's seen his phone.

b. He thinks that his boxer shorts are

"meowing" because he hasn't seen his cat in weeks.

c. It could be featured on the cover of "Better Homes and Slums."

~

What's the difference between a man and a monkey?

The monkey can be trained to take out the garbage.

~

Science has discovered that most living things require a clean environment. There are some exceptions however, such as bacteria, common molds, and men.

~

My husband never puts his clothes away. Our kids grew up thinking doorknobs were made of dacron polyester.

~

What do you know about a man who wears a wrinkled, stained shirt to work?

His wife's out of town.

~

Asking a husband to keep half the bedroom clean is:

a. impossible

b. like talking to your teenager

c. like asking the pigeons to clean up the statues

~

Usually the last time a man's bed is made is when it was made in the factory.

~

Men are incredible slobs. If we could just get them to pick up their dirty socks, we could eliminate half the toxic waste dumps in America.

~

A husband takes off a dirty shirt. He will

a. drop it on the floor.

b. complain if there are any wrinkles.

c. expect it to be clean the next day.

d. all of the above

~

Men never pick up after themselves. If a single man drops something on the floor, it lies there until he gets married and his wife picks it up for him.

~

The average bachelor lives in an apartment that is so sloppy:

a. it would look like it's been burglarized except that burglars don't make that much of a mess.

b. he could apply for money from an earthquake victims relief fund and probably get it.

c. the mere sight of it would give Mother Theresa a tension headache.

~

MY GUY

~

My boyfriend says to me, "I want it, I want it tonight, and I want it at least 5 times." He was talking about beer.

~

My guy insists he's a workaholic. I keep telling him that to be one, he actually has to work.

~

My guy tells me he has hidden charms, but they're so well hidden, I've never been able to find them.

~

Overweight? When he goes to the beach, he struts his stuffing.

~

Lazy? He was stranded for three hours after a power failure... on an escalator!

~

What are his friends like? Well, he saw "Revenge of the Nerds"- and thought it was a documentary.

~

I found an economical way to double my closet space. I got rid of my boyfriend.

~

I wouldn't say he's handsome, suave and debonair. I wouldn't, but he would.

~

I'd like to bring him home to mother- *his* mother.

~

My boyfriend's well balanced- he's got a chip on *both* shoulders.

~

He's the kind of guy who would give you the shirt off someone else's back.

~

When I'm with my man, my pulse races, I tremble all over, my palms sweat... he has got to be the world's weirdest driver!

~

My guy is so used to cheating. One time we were playing golf and he got a hole in one, so he marked down zero.

~

HABITS

~

It wasn't enough for men to annoy us 16 hours a day. God had to make it a clean sweep by adding snoring.

~

What are the 3 most unlikely things in the world?

Madonna marrying the Pope, Bullwinkle eloping with the Queen, and a man stopping to ask directions.

~

I shouldn't complain about my husband

watching sports on TV. If it weren't for the 7th inning stretch, I wouldn't have any sex life at all!

~

Men are naturally competitive. Even in the Garden of Eden, Adam was afraid Eve would like the snake's fruit better than his.

~

A man is thinking about a birthday present for his lady. He will:

a. wait until the last minute to buy it

b. ignore any hints she has dropped

c. buy the wrong size, color and style.

~

What's the best way to have your husband remember your anniversary?

Get married on his birthday.

~

Why do balding men comb their hair across their heads?

So they can fool themselves.

~

Why do men brag they still have the first dollar they ever earned, when they can't hold on to any of the subsequent ones?

~

Men learn distrust very early in life. I think it starts at the circumcision when the doctor leans over and says, "This won't hurt a bit!"

~

WOMEN

~

What does P.M.S. really stand for?

PUTTING UP WITH MEN'S SHIT!!!

~

Why are women beginning to like work better than sex?

More perks, and the pay is better.

~

What has convinced a lot of women to believe in divorce?

Marriage.

~

Why would it be better if a marriage license were like a business license?

We women could just let it expire.

~

Most women find their men aren't as interested in sex after marriage. In some marriages, the situation is so bad that:

a. after years of marriage, the couple can *still* qualify for an annulment.

b. the husband really is reading *Playboy* just for the articles.

c. Kim Basinger had more sex in "9 1/2 Weeks" than these couples have in 9 1/2 years!

~

Most women are satisfied with their husbands- they've had all they want of them!

~

Why do women have a higher threshold of pain?

We need it to put up with men.

~

BREAKING UP

~

Men are so wrapped up in their work, that when you want to reject a man, it helps if you use the very same key words he uses on the job. *Those* words he *will* understand. Here are some examples:

If he's a...	**SAY, "Our relationship has...**
banker/accountant	...gone bankrupt."
race car driver	...run it's course."
personnel worker	...been terminated."
boxer	...been K.O.'d."

miner	...gone bust."
soldier	...been wiped out."
opera star	...reached its grand finale."
milkman	...gone sour."
bus driver	...reached the end of the line."

~

EXs

~

The Census is wrong- they counted my ex as a human being.

~

He always liked to live up to a certain standard- the double standard.

~

The Surgeon General says the best way to have safe sex is to have no sex at all. With my ex, this was easy to do.

~

I hear my ex is trying to find himself. When he does, he'll find a lazy idiot!

~

He was trying to find himself when we were married too. I used to tell him he could work while he's looking.

~

How is an ex-husband like an inflamed appendix?

It caused you a lot of pain, and after it was removed you found out you didn't need it anyway.

~

He wants to be on TV, but he never will be unless it's "America's Least Wanted."

~

BACKWARDS JOKES

~

A: A mental hospital.

Q: Where do you have to go to find a committed man?

~

A: About an hour.

Q: What's the difference between a husband and a lover?

~

A: A few good men.

Q: What are the women of America and the Marine Corps both having trouble finding?

~

A: Dirty Harry

Q: How does Harry look when he shows up for a date?

~

A: Three Men and a Baby

Q: What do you get when four men go fishing and one doesn't catch anything?

~

A: "Let's stop and ask for directions."

Q: What sentence is never spoken by a man?

~

A: The last laugh.

Q: What is alimony?

~

A: Toast and coffee.

Q: What are the only two things a man can cook without help?

~

A: The parting of the Red Sea, water turned into wine, and a man who mows the lawn voluntarily.

Q: Name 3 miracles.

~

Would you like to see
your favorite joke(s) about men
in print?

If so, send them to:

Cindy Garner
c/o Newport House
107 R.R. 620, Suite 7-A
Austin, TX 78734

No credit or compensation can be given,
and only those funny enough
will be included.